IN LOVE WITH PAIN

V E N T U M

Dedication

Let me
tell you what
makes my heart
feel really heavy.
This is for all the ones,
who lost their lives because
of useless wars, all the ones
whose chapters were filled
with *blood* , instead of *love.*

Warning

Spoiler:

This book doesn't have a happy ending .

WHEN THE NIGHT COMES

The night comes, and the monster in me awakes. I put on a mask and simply call him ventum. This is when the moon cannot save me and the sun is on the other side, when stars are nothing but stars. When the dark tears me apart, I sit there asking: What makes me numb? What makes me depressed? From the outside, it looks like a boy holding a pen, putting on a smile, but the mask lies. Within me, the soul cries, and the more I think, the more I write, the more I hurt, the more I feel alive. My mind gets dark and deep. I pick up words and put them into poems. These are the secrets he and I keep, we become one, and the more we write, the less we sleep. This is where he takes over and becomes my voice in my silence. This is when all I have ever been meets the little boy, the man, the lover, the hurter, and the monster, all in one, in the darkest, most terrible place you'll ever find. This is when I find comfort in all of the chaos, in the darkness. He might be a monster, but maybe I am too. Maybe he became me—perhaps I am the mask and he is me—but whatever he is, this is, it saves me, because despite all these dark nights, he's the one that left a light on.

GLIMPSES

come in, I'll show you
a glimpse of my soul,
a glimpse of my heart—
where it starts bleeding,
where wounds become scars,
and where I hide my feelings.
come in, I'll show my wars,
I'll show you my mind.
it's a very dark place.
I'll show you where
the poems are made.
it's a very numb,
empty, and lost space.
come in, and I'll show you
what I've become—
too broken for many,
yet loved by some.

THE YOUNG WRITER

in love with pain
were the first words
a young writer once
put on paper, and
I wish I could go back
and tell him to stop,
that he will never
find the balance
between love and pain,
that he will be forever
caught within an old soul
and a very young heart.
I wish I could go back
and tell him that he will be
lost and never find himself,
that I am terrified he will eventually
become a writer, and nothing else.

LOST

I am lost,
numb inside.
I choose to hide
in a sea of ink
where I have
been drowning
over many years.
Find me
in the depths
of these waters,
where love lies
on the ground,
where I don't
fear being lost,
but being found.

WHEN I WRITE

there is a child
living in my heart,
and in the silence,
when it skips a beat,
you can hear him whisper,
stop, we are not safe.
this is when I put on a mask,
rip myself and words apart,
when I open up these scars,
when they are within,
not seen but felt.
stop, we are not safe.
this is when suffering does
not wear a name or face.
when I rip words apart,
rip them in two,
he whispers, *stop,*
and with every word,
I rip a part of him too.

OLD SOUL

I am an old soul.
love is what i have,
and what i don't.
carry it within,
deep within,
but perhaps it is,
too much
for this world.
that's why
I don't have it.
I see love,
and I carry it within
as the thing it is
pure rawness,
and this is why
I don't fit in.
I am a too old a soul
in a too-young world.

TWO MOMENTS, A BEAT

I exist in
two seconds,
two moments,
within a beat,
within a skip.
this is how I love.
this is what I am,
this where I exist.
within an ordinary beat,
and a skip of madness.

DREAMER

I am a dreamer,
neither lost nor found,
waiting for a story
worth dreaming forever.

HEARTS & SOULS

I walk
on the ashes
of my heart
because I carry
the fire in my soul.
hearts become ashes;
souls burn forever.

LONELY

being surrounded by many
was the loneliest
chapter in my life.

CURSED, BLESSED

I want to destroy you,
I want to ruin you.
pure madness isn't it?
as deep as I love,
as deep I can hurt,
as imperfect I am,
as perfect I can be—
I am a total mess,
a beautiful disaster,
cursed and blessed,
worthy of love,
worthy of hate.

2:27 A.M. | FEARS

I don't have many of them, but let's talk about the silly fears I had as a child. Like thunder. I was always scared of it. If there was a storm, I couldn't sleep the whole night. That changed when I grew up, though. I love the rain and storms, but that's another story. My fears changed when I grew up, thanks to love. I didn't have as many fears in the beginning of adulthood. Then pain cut deep. First, I developed a fear of losing, then I became jealous. And at some point, I feared love. I wish I could say that changed, like my fear of thunder, but some storms hold on longer. Dammit, already five minutes gone. It's 2:32 a.m. now. I probably should go to sleep. Oh wait. There is this fear which—but wait, I am not ready for that. Let's leave that out. I have a fear of losing my parents, which is normal, I guess. Related to family, I feared not having one of my own once. I am a simple guy. I've never wanted to be famous. I just want to be known by one person, and I often fear I won't be. Four minutes gone again. It's 2:36 a.m. now, which makes me go to my last and biggest fear.

You know what they say, "time is the only thing we have, and don't." Such a painful thought, to think you never know how much you have left. As I said, I don't fear death, but I fear time. I fear time so much. Why? Because we can't control it. Nobody can. It doesn't matter who you are, how much you have, what you've done, good or bad—time doesn't wait. As I said, I don't have many fears, but it's already 2:40 a.m., and I should really sleep now. Just a note, while I lost about fifteen minutes by writing this, you lost some too while reading or even re-reading it, which was a waste. You lost a bit of time, and I can't give it back to you. Nobody can. Some stories are pointless to read twice, some lovers don't deserve a second chance, and some friends don't deserve it either. Time doesn't wait, time doesn't say, "Okay, let's stop and try again." It doesn't choose the crowds you are surrounded by; it just fades away, and it never comes back, but all the things that time doesn't do, you can. I can't give the time back to you, but what I can do is change my lost time into words that may change your mind-set and hopefully have a positive effect.

HOPE

suffering today,
loving the very next.

LIFE

life is just a moment
between birth and death,
just a deep, deep breath
full of dreams and memories.

TIME

a word that turns even stars into dust.

WASTED YOUTH

What I had wrapped in my hands was the youth that slipped away, as it was never mine. I am afraid to say that I have wasted too many years trying to make them happy while building a prison of thoughts in my mind, a cage I could never escape. I realized it but too late, and I wished I wasted that youth more on smiles and laughs. But I didn't, and that's why I hold nothing today but a key to my prison. What I hold tightly today is not my youth but my wisdom.

FRAGILE

my heart is too fragile.
just a bit of love,
just a bit of a shake,
is all it'd take,
to make it break
and break and break.

TOO MUCH

I often feel
too much,
but sometimes
I feel everything
all at once,
and that's where
my heart almost
falls apart.

SOMETIMES

love stole all the
breath from my lungs.
I tried not to feel,
gasping after air,
but this pain was
breathtaking too.

"LISTEN"

I
hear
jealousy
whispering,
this
lying
manipulative
asshole.

ALMOST

this is my war,
I let it come close,
but it never kills me,
so it ends as it
always does—
almost.

IF I WOULD ASK YOU

Does pain make you, or do you make it? Would you choose between them, or would you choose both like me? I made it, and it made me. Life isn't just about love, but pain as well. Both of them go hand in hand. And this is the whole beautiful, terrifying chaos about it; sometimes I can control the pain, and sometimes I can't. I have realized that I eventually never heal but just keep it within me. I've learned to live with it. To go with it. To just let it be. I found comfort in the pain. And in the end, pain is just a thing I choose to feed, and love is a thing I often seek. The only difference is they don't exist at the same time. When one is awake, and when the other is asleep.

LOVE

you are alive—
breathing doesn't mean
just a gasp of air.
love sometimes is
much more than that—
and often it isn't.

PAIN
(read from the bottom)

A SAD STORY

I caught
my heart breaking
while I was smiling.
such a shame.

THE IRONY

love, a lover's death.

LIVING FOREVER

there is this
very tragic story
about two lovers,
where the girl says,
dying young is beautiful;
they'll remember you that way.
but the boy
feared losing her,
so he made her the muse,
and the world should know it,
she lived forever,
and he died the day
he became the poet.

I DON'T CHASE STARS

Isn't it foolish,
how I write about
stars all my life
but never chase them?
it would be if I could,
but I can't chase stars.
I could dedicate all
the time I have, and
I wouldn't even make
it near to them, and
even if I could they
would burn me alive.
but I can sit in the darkness
and suffer among them,
accepting that chasing them
would be the death of me.
I would chase a love
that never can be.
so these are what's left,
the night and the
beautiful view that
make my heart
break in two.
I can't chase stars,
I can't chase you.

TOXIC

when I loved,
it wasn't enough.
when I was there
all the time,
it wasn't enough.
when I was the
best of me,
it wasn't enough.
I choose to,
hurt you,
destroy you,
break you.
so when I finally
had enough and left,
you came back,
just because
I was once
like them.

THE HEARTBREAK

I have come to
realize that mornings
destroy me the most.
right after I wake up
is when I feel numb.

KILL ME

you said, *it is what it is.*
and I wake up every morning,
putting this right on my lips,
next to the coffee that is today
too creamy to remind me of
your dark brown eyes,
which just makes me
take a deeper breath,
and it seems as though hope
burns to ashes with
every inhale,
and I keep hearing,
you need to stop—
it's going to kill you,
but I keep inhaling,
even though it steals my breath.
this is what makes me feel alive.
all that is left is this,
everything I put on my lips.
it's as if death gives me a kiss,
but I guess it is what it is.

— *the cigarettes and you*

SUN AND MOON

there is a story
about these two
that the world isn't
brave enough to write.
the moon is
cold and hurting,
while the sun is in
his pain, burning.
and once in a while
they meet, but too rarely
to call it love.
so, the world
calls those moments
eclipses instead,
moon and sun
trying to collide
while we just
see a red light.
and perhaps,
they almost do.
but they never will,
and the saddest part
about these two:
they never knew.

SWEET LIPS

I fear lips
that taste like honey
but speak bitterly.

IN THE MORNING

before the dawn,
I watch the moon disappear.
knowing what is next,
it reminds me
too much of you.
and despite what
we've been through,
I can't wait to feel
the sun burn my skin,
yet I hate it deep within.
I am sick of the sun
for it burned me
like you did.

DROWNING

all I heard was
drown, drown, drown.
all I heard was
remember to breathe.
tell me,
did I ever have a chance?
still waters run deep,
and you were the
whole damn ocean.

BIRD SET FREE

just because
you let a bird
out of a cage
doesn't mean
it is free.
perhaps
there is a
bigger cage.

FEATHER IN THE WIND

As years went by, I always thought I was a lost feather caught within the forces of the air. I thought that love came in the blowing wind, because this is what I was always told. I can't control it. I am too lost, too hard to love. But I found out that my love is wild, and when you try to tame it, I get destructive. I am all the forces that can't be controlled, that seek to be free. I am not lost; in fact, you lost me. I am the love you will seek, but also the one you will never find, for you tried to control the feather, but I was always the wind.

STARDUST

at the end,
I never left pieces,
but always dust.
you will remember me,
for the star I was,
burning for love,
and you will see
not everyone can be.

AT OTHER TIMES

I think of death
and my breath is calm,
knowing I will find peace.
that makes me think
of you and the moment
you left. something in me
was dying, but my breath
was calm, because I knew
there would be peace after you.

DEPTH

I have the depth of a universe in me,
but you never looked at the skies anyway.

ALL YOU EVER WANTED

there it was,
all you ever wanted,
my heart begging
having so much to say,
there it was,
all you ever wanted,
leaving rather than to stay.

NOT MEANT TO BE

what we lacked,
was the rhyme.
when i was the night,
you were the day,
and when you
were the light,
I was darkness.
but if we had said
words differently,
like *you are the light*
and I am the night.

—the rhyme was missing.

THE BIRD

When I was a child, we found a newborn bird in the garden. Sadly, the mother was dead, so we took him in our house and read about how to care for it. We made him a nest in the beginning when he couldn't fly yet. After a few weeks, he started to fly a bit, so we bought him a cage but let him fly around a few times a day. After he got too big, we let him out to be free. I don't know if this is painful or beautiful, but even when set free, he always came back and slept on our windows. He was always around, and perhaps this is love. Once you've really felt it, you never let it go.

HOME

I wandered
on the edges
of the galaxies
half a universe away
just to find out
nothing leads me to you.

DANCING WITH YOUR GHOST

and there i was
on this empty street,
under all the lights,
dancing into the night
and for all its stars,
and for a moment,
just for a moment,
you were there.

SWEET & BITTER

I wonder,
were you bitter to them,
or were you sweet
and they tasted bitter?
if so, that's funny because
I turned bitter, and that
made me think of you.
I wonder, as you turned
sweet and they hurt you,
did I cross your mind too?

SLEEP

the beat of your heart
does not sing me
to sleep anymore.

ECHOES

in the most
silent moments,
when the heart
is the loudest,
you can hear
the feelings
that never left,
like echoes
that come back.

ONCE IN A WHILE

we feel it all again
when we get caught
by the feelings
we left behind,
when a thought
becomes a smile.
in the end we were just
lovers that crossed
each other's mind
once in a while.

LOOKS

we fall
for what we see.
even though
the universe has
an endless depth,
we choose,
too often,
the beauty
of the moon
as to discover the
depth of a soul.

HELL, AND HEAVEN

Sometimes you fall in love and there is so much fire that hearts and souls burn, that kissing feels like a storm of fire taking over and touching skin burns your hands. There is just so much fire that loving someone hurts like hell. And eventually, two become one. This is when love becomes a whole mess. One day you are cold, the other day burning, because of passion. This is when lovers become sinners—caught in each other's hell, and heaven.

FIRE

they say don't play with it,
but a glimpse at the flames
that set our souls on fire,
turned them cold, too.

— *so, what were we playing with?*

SINNER

you have heaven
in your smile,
hell in your eyes.
looking at you burns
my heart and skin.
you are a devilish lover
and my most loved sin.

KNOWN TO BE COLD

she was known
to be cold, but
she was more
known to burn
for the ones
that set her
soul on fire.

BURNED SKIN

her skin tastes as if
she walked on fire.
she's an angel and
one hell of a lover.

THE BURNING ANGEL

she's caught between
hell, and heaven—
a cold heart and
flames in her soul,
smile of an angel,
mind of the devil.

FLAMES

she never wanted to
run away from the past.
she wasn't meant to
rise out of the ashes.
she rather walked on them,
with wings on flames and
a smile, as if she was
the one burning it all down

THE SIN

we wanted to love
each other so much
that when the other didn't,
we still tried.

TWO LOVERS

but
in the end
we were two lovers
in hell and paradise,
making sins in the name of love,
growing a desire to burn passionately in fire.

BEAUTIFUL

What she had been through never really bothered her. Even though the world often didn't love her, it was the world she fell hopelessly in love with. She knew nothing should be taken for granted and appreciated everything that came to her. Even when she was hurting, she let it hurt until it went away. She was the most peace I have known, and she walked in all of it, as if she was just an ordinary girl. But she was the most beautiful, not in just how she looked, but in how she thought.

HER MIND

her mind is the
most beautiful place.
it is where
walls are too high
and nobody gets in;
where old meets young
and soul meets heart;
where both pairs collide to one,
and she collects those
moments and memories from
a playground full of dreams;
where the woman meets the girl
and plays with the broken pieces
as if they were never broken—
they can hurt her, break her,
but they can't take away
the peace she lives in.
they can break the woman,
but they can't break the girl.

FREEDOM

she   fly.
    fell   to
        and   began
            fell   then
                but

WILDFLOWER

her heart is never
in the same place,
but do not mistake
that with loving less.
she's everchanging
and grows in places
too wild, too free.

HER

storm in her eyes, peace in her smile.

ALL STORMS

she could be both,
the madness
of a hurricane
or the peace
of the wind.
she is a mess,
a beautiful mess.
all storms were.

SHE'S

she's a perfect mess,
a beautiful disaster,
chaos within tragedy.

ART

she never fit, in the eyes
of the world, but tell me,
how could someone
who found comfort
in the disaster,
beauty in the chaos,
peace in the broken pieces—
how could someone
who was meant to be art,
a masterpiece of tragedy—
tell me, how could she fit
in the eyes of the ones
who did not feel?

SHE NEVER MADE SENSE

she's beautifully
out of this world,
belonging to dreams,
breathing stories
we can't get
from this poem.
beautifully out of place,
it never made sense.
she never made sense.

MADE OF FAIRYTALES

oh darling,
show them your eyes
and the fairytales within—
the dragons and all that's tragic.
show them your smile—
the world loves magic.

TELL US ABOUT HER

the world said,
and there I was, left
writing endless poems.
because how do you
explain the universe
to someone who just
belongs in it? How do
you explain the stars
to the ones who've never
touched the sky?

UNIVERSE

she leaves
dust of her heart
everywhere she goes.
she's at peace
with the universe
in her mind
that has the
depth of the galaxies,
with a soul in the
shades of dark,
eyes full of stars.

HALF OF IT

she always gave away,
half of the moon—
that's how she
outplayed them.
she knew there
was an entire
galaxy to discover.

ROSES

the summer left
and autumn came,
so she picked up
the roses of the love
they had left behind.
love comes with thorns,
love comes with pain.
they all left storms,
but she was meant
to dance in the rain.

HER SMILE

is beautifully terrifying.
its where she reveals
sadness and happiness,
and it just doesn't make sense.

THE STARS

I've always wondered
whether the stars get jealous
of how bright you shine
on these dark nights.

WITHIN HERSELF

is a peace that lives in
the form of an old soul
and the wildness within the beat
of a very young heart.
she lives and loves with
the depth of the mind,
the rawness of her love.
and I wonder if she sees
all the things that I see—
poetry in how she is,
young, beautiful, and free.

AS FREE AS THE OCEAN

let her be free, or she will
drown you within her depths,
where beautiful waves are,
and where its catastrophic.
the waves of today can be
the tsunamis of tomorrow.

WAVES

the ocean
you once knew
became a sea.
she lost some
of her depth
but found peace
in the still waters,
and she is never
coming back.

NATURE

she's rain and wind,
peace and wild combined.

DEAR, SOULMATE

I don't know you, neither do I know if we are similar
or made of the same things. But I do know,
the universe, will push us towards each other,
but till then I can just imagine, how you look like,
how you feel like and I wonder if your hair will
be straight, curly or just a bit wavy, how soft your
skin, and tender your voice will be. If you have
dimples next to your smile, or freckles beneath your
eyes. I wonder, if they look like all the places
I never been. And yet all of this doesn't matter,
to how breathtaking your love must be, that just a
gasp of air, must feel like forever. The rhythm of
your heart must be the perfect symphony to mine,
looking at you, must feel like the universe, dancing
to words, galaxies turning into poems. This is what
you must be, the peace, calming the war within.

A LETTER

to the women,
I haven't met yet,
I don't know
where you live,
but I do know
where you exist:
on the edge
of these letters,
on white paper,
within the space
where the ink is
separated and the
melancholy stops,
where breaths of
hope are taken
in the space of bliss.
I don't know where you live,
but where you exist is this.

ALL THIS TIME

tell that little thing
within your chest that
I want to listen to all
the secrets it has to tell,
that I want to know
why it is broken,
where it goes wild,
where it finds peace.
tell that little thing
that I want it how it is,
how it stops and goes,
tell that little thing,
there is a place next to mine,
and it's been waiting for it
all this time.

WHAT IS LOVE?

A question I might never answer right, or with an explanation that makes sense. But it appears to me that we often mistake love for just a feeling. The reality is, the feelings in the beginning will not last forever. Eventually they will get weaker, or you just get used to it, and this is where there is this big difference in feeling and loving. I don't know—I may be completely out of place with this—but I think that lots of us concentrate too much on feelings. When the blinding effects of the feelings stop, many lover's assume that's when love stops. Really, this is where love begins. Feelings were always just roots that grow into a trunk with branches. This happens when a relationship is about communication mutual respect, acceptance, selflessness, teamwork, trust, and so on. Perhaps love doesn't exist in the form we think it does. Maybe it never was a feeling but the whole picture. It's not about the roots, the trunk, or the branches—but all that together. I think this is what love really is. This is where it starts: when the blindness stops, and it isn't about the roots but the whole tree.

YOU AND ME

such a wild and rebellious act of love.

LOVE

we were fools,
falling for smiles
and laughter—
fools
for the
very thing
that made
us think
that love,
only love,
stops time.

THE LOVER, THE KILLER

in a matter of seconds
before bullets of love hit me,
right before your finger slips,
before it breaks my bones
right through my skin,
I become the lover,
and you the killer.
this is when
my heart begs,
smile again—
pull the trigger.

SOULMATES

we smile
at each other
when our hearts skip,
laugh when it starts,
lovers with broken souls
and laughing hearts.

CONSTELLATIONS

I feel lost.

oh darling,
that's how stars love.

SOMETIMES

love is falling,
trying to fly,
but oh boy,
once you fly...

A FEW, A LITTLE

all we want is
a few smiles,
a few laughs,
a little bit of rain,
a little bit of sun,
a few little moments
to live, to love.

BLOOMING

once we set seeds
we don't bother to
go somewhere else.
all we need is water,
and it blows my mind
how we are like flowers
that just wait to bloom
with someone else's love.

TWO WORLDS

two worlds
falling apart,
colliding into one—
love is such a disaster.

HOLDING YOU

I am the hand
that holds you
when your world
breaks in two.

HORIZON

in a time
where love seems
to have no depth,
you sit there in the
shallow of the seas,
asking how you could
fall for me.
I share
the weakness of
the sun and moon.
when you smile,
when you laugh,
as love can
make you do,
is when I fall
for the ocean
that is you.

FOREVER

some walk on love
as if they are
a shooting star
burning out
between galaxies,
and I wonder if this is
what forever feels like—

just a second.

ECLIPSE

when they kissed,
one was beneath the sun,
the other beneath the moon,
they collided with lips,
and their world turned
into a total eclipse.

WAVES

love comes in waves,
and we were just
waiting like grains of sand
to be taken into the depths.

DRUNK POET

every time
you told yourself,
I am not enough,
it was as you filled these
words into an empty bottle.
this is when you made me
completely drunk in love.
poems never tasted as good,
and I was always too drunk
to explain how much
you really were.

LETTING GO

Don't let it go. Hold onto it. Let it hurt. The truth is, you can't choose either way. Fighting it will create an even bigger war. Don't reverse progress that has already been made because there is nothing like just letting go and being free. Whoever says otherwise is lying. You need to feel pain as you feel love. And that will hurt. You will feel numb, sometimes more, sometimes less, and on some days, you will laugh and feel joy. And when you think, *finally, it's going to get better*, it comes back, and destroys you in ways you thought words, memories, and moments never could. Breathing will seem like a challenge. You'll feel weak because healing seems like such a weak thing to do. This will go on for weeks and months, and it will feel like forever, and even then, you never will be the same as before. I think if someone leaves, a big part of us will leave with them, and I think you never truly heal. You learn to live with it. It won't hurt, but you will always remember. That's when wounds become scars. But don't let it go. Let it hurt. Growth starts not with forgetting but accepting.

THE FIGHT

if you catch your heart and mind at war,
it is your worth, the mind is fighting for.

MISTAKEN

you have
mistaken me
for a love to just
keep around,
but you don't
just keep
flowers around
and then ask
why they aren't
growing.

PATIENCE

love me
with patience.
I wasn't born
without a heart.
I am not cold.
I am still learning
to feel it again.
maybe not tonight, but
perhaps tomorrow,
I'll find the light.

BLAME

there is a time
when you hurt,
there is a time
when you heal,
there is a time
when you feel,
but there is never
a wrong time.
do not blame
a decision on time.

LEAVING LOVE

some leave love,
and with that
they leave hope.

TOO LATE

I am afraid
to say we already
have planted seeds
from which our children
will reap poison.

WORST KIND

the worst kind of people
are the ones who push you
to the edge of a cliff but
never far enough to let you fall.

LOVE IS NOT A GAME

but if it is,
and you are playing,
you are already losing.

HOW OFTEN CAN A HEART BREAK?

as often as you let it.

WHEN THEY LEAVE

you break the most
when people leave,
because it is as if a
piece of you leaves too.

THE WORLD ENDS

not when the heart breaks,
but when the soul does.

POISON

don't search for love in hate;
you won't find life in a
sea filled with poison.

WOUNDS

sometimes
they cut too deep
to forgive or forget.

ITS NOT

don't tell
yourself
it's love.
you being
hurt is not
how they love.
it's just you hurting.

POWER

women like you
turn winds into
entire storms,
and yet you ask,
am I enough.

THINGS CHANGE

when you become
enough for yourself
and too much for them.

BALANCE

nothing breaks like a heart,
but nothing heals as one.

ALL, HALF, NOTHING

it's okay
to feel it all.
it's okay
to feel half,
or nothing at all.

—*the moon isn't always full.*

BETTER

often
there is a much
better love,
a much bigger
picture
than what you
have the
pieces for
right now.

BRAVE

you trust your vulnerability,
and yet you ask how to be strong.

—a hell of a plot twist

LET IT HURT

let rivers flow in you;
that's how you heal
and eventually
find the way out.

AGAIN AND AGAIN

that's life—we live,
love, and fly,
and if all that
doesn't work now,
tomorrow we try.

LONG & SHORT

this is us in a long story or at the end of a short
poem. to all the beautiful ones who wonder,
is he writing about me or about someone
special. I am writing to all of us, to me, to you,
because some of us were left alone in pain.
it's an absolute mess—no, it's much more. it's
different and an absolute disaster. it's in chaos
from how they left us—oh, and from all
the ways they hurt us. but, dear, rest,
rest, because you been through too much.
but don't forget how to live in this pain. life is
so beautiful. there is more than we know. we
are just grains of sand in all the waves—
you, me, everyone is meant to be
special in someone's story. one day you will be,
and trust me, one day love will feel so
different from all the poems you know, different
from all the stories this world has told you until now.
the love in you will once be set free. until then,
rest. because you been through too much.

I LOST YOU

in the place
where love
once grew

AND

in the pieces
that were not
enough for you.

I FOUND ME.

who would've
thought losing you,
would set me free.

BUT DEAR

there is sun after rain, love after pain.

WEAKNESS

hurting seems like
such a weak thing to do,
but the truth is
you are in a process
of healing from a love
you felt too much.

OVERTHINKING

you'll break,
fall apart,
and when you do,
you'll overthink it.
it will feel like drowning
within a sea.
but trust me,
you'll heal.
first you drown,
but then you'll be free.

WOUNDS BECOME SCARS

that's when you
don't hurt anymore.
you heal, but you'll
always remember.
and that's okay.
growth starts
not with forgetting
but with accepting.

LIFE AND THE STORIES

Don't think you have already written some lines, filled some of the pages, or even ended a few chapters. The reality is you didn't even start writing. This book doesn't start when you are born or with the first heartbreak or first love. Everything up to now doesn't matter if beauty or pain are always outside the book. Your book doesn't start with all of this; it starts when all of what was makes sense.

SELF-LOVE

there are so many people to love,
but the best one is always
you.

I HOPE

you get lost
in yourself and
that it is self-love,
you find within,
that after a while,
you look in the mirror,
with your pretty eyes
and your cheeky smile.

SAME FACE

once you
fall in love
with yourself,
they will get
a glimpse of life
on the exact same face
that was struggling to smile.
that's when the world
falls in love with you.

OH DARLING

love will come
as if the sun
was never gone.

RIVERS

like rivers,
we end up
where we
always were
meant to go.

LET YOUR HEART KNOW

as long as it beats,
as long as it feels,
it is alive.
you are alive.
and as long
there is life,
there is love,
there is hope,
there is you.

CHAPTERS?

I thought to put this book in chapters, but why? Life doesn't work in chapters. You heal today, hurt tomorrow, or hurt today and heal tomorrow. It doesn't work in falling, loving hurting and at the end, healing. Sometimes you fall but don't love, or you hurt for a long, long time till you feel a release. Sometimes you heal and don't fall for many years. Often, all this repeats over and over again You can't just turn the page and move on. The truth isn't that simple. Sometimes you will feel more, sometimes less. It takes a damn long time to go through it, and you will change along the way. That is part of growing, so why should I put walls between who I was and who I am? All that was is still a part of me and always will be. Sometimes it is about finding comfort in the mess, not ordering it. That's why I decided to make this book a whole mess, because in the end, it is a mirror of my soul and heart.

POETRY

love from the broken.

LOVE STORY

the reader and the writer
must be the deepest, wildest
love story that was never told.

WRITING

putting it on
paper is a relief,
the writer said.
this is when
I was shocked,
in disbelief, thinking,
I must be a poet then.

OLD & YOUNG

I believe souls are old,
and hearts are young,
that's why we break easy.

TO YOUNG WRITERS

Before you pick up the pen and put it on paper, I want you to know that there is no such thing as the perfect prose or the perfect poems. I want you to know that there will be things that someone already said, already wrote, already used, but it's not about the words; it's about the voice that says them, the mind that thinks them, the heart that feels them. I don't have many things to say about how to start writing. Just know that by taking this step, you are walking into eternity; think about what you write, what you say, what you use. A writer's first words, first lyrics, first poem can be something great. It can be a voice that nobody has ever heard but always needed to listen to. Words are the most powerful weapon every human has within. Without words, there wouldn't be actions. You never know how much of a difference a few words, can make to a soul, a heart, or even the world. You never know how great your words can be, how great you can be. If you have something to say, write it. Write it loud

WORDS

it's funny what words can do.
sometimes the things we say
keep us t
            o
              g
                e
                  t
                    h
                      e
                        r

                    or they make us fall apart.

often, we are like parallel lines,
close but never together

and sometimes
we are so close,
evenwordscollide.

BAD HABITS

writers have a bad habit
of keeping stories alive
that have long ended.

TO BE FELT

and one day
we will be wise.
we will realize
love never had
to make sense,
just be felt.

ADDICTED

I am going to tell you
a secret about writers.
There are two of us:
the ones with love,
and the ones with the pain
and drugs we loved dying for.

THE READERS

I have found that
women are often
unafraid to show
they are hurting.
they are often
the loud readers.
they share it,
show it to the world,
show their strength,
and then
there is a minority
that hurts in silence,
the silent readers
I call "men".

STORIES

I believe
we die
many times
in our lives,
most often
while reading
or writing.
I believe
at the end
of a story
the writer and
the reader die.

THINGS POETS DON'T WRITE

There are things nobody wants to say, that love can be an ugly thing. That you'll hurt a long time and won't fully heal from it. That there is quite a pain that will follow you day and night. That you just cannot let go that easily. There are poems we don't want to write: That the moon is gone more often than that it is full. That the sun is just another star of many. That the universe could have an end. That storms are not always beautiful (and usually just destroy). That the ocean is not endless. That flowers don't last forever, and that roses are more painful than beautiful. That chaos is a terrible thing and being a mess was never healthy for a relationship. That wildness was never good for lovers. That life is not forever. These are all the things writers don't dare to write. Because writers fear reality. Writers are just kids, living in their own imaginations, far away from reality, and readers just pay for the show.

WHEN I BITE THE DUST

words live forever,
that's why I write
because with my
last breath
all of me,
is this.

ONE DAY

with my last breath,
I will be known for
being foolish or wise.
it will leave the
world speechless,
or they will be
disgusted at me for
saying love is pain and
life is nothing but death.
for being a broken soul
with a laughing heart,
for falling in love with pain,
I'll be a fool for many,
or wise for some.
although all
of this was tough,
I never lived and loved
quite enough.

BE KIND

a moment or a smile can let others breathe.

A MOMENT

Little moments where a few words and a little conversation makes you smile are what life is about. I live for these things; this is why I want to tell you about a person I met last night who made me smile in a moment when I was struggling. I hope that whenever you are struggling with anything, this makes you smile too. This page is dedicated to you, the girl who cut her dolls open at a young age in order to become a doctor. I believe in you.

LAST WORDS

there is an end
to everything
the world whispers.
perhaps
the universe answers
in a sarcastic manner.

THE END

there is no happy endling,
but there is this.
this moment.
two strangers,
you and me,
sharing a moment,
through this book.
I hope
I made you
smile, cry, feel.
perhaps this is
the meaning of life,
little moments like this.
to smile, to cry, to feel.
perhaps this is it.
this moment.
this perfect ending.

LATIN

DEFINITIONEM VENTUM

1. a tempestate
2. impetus tempestatis
3. motus aeris
4. anfractibus vel circularis vel habere directionem
5. vim vi perniciosa

ENGLISH

DEFINITION OF WIND

1. a storm
2. a hurricane
3. air in natural motion
4. to have a circular or spiral course or direction
5. a destructive force or influence